Preface

The world is changing faster than ever. In the midst of economic turbulence, technological disruption, and shifting geopolitical landscapes, one innovation continues to stand out: Bitcoin.

Through the use of AI technology, I created *The Bitcoin Pocket Book* as a clear, concise, and comprehensive guide to understanding the Bitcoin revolutionary technology. Whether you are completely new to Bitcoin, an investor seeking to deepen your conviction, or a professional integrating digital assets into your strategy, this book provides actionable insights, timeless principles, and a grounded understanding of:

- Why Bitcoin was created and how it works

- The flaws in modern money and banking systems

- Wealth-building strategies tailored to Bitcoin's unique nature

- The philosophical, social, and ethical implications of decentralized money

- Practical tools and indicators for navigating Bitcoin markets

- The real-world impacts and global movement surrounding Bitcoin

This book is organized into 21 structured chapters, designed for reading sequentially or referencing individually as needed. Each chapter distills key concepts without unnecessary jargon, aiming to spark your curiosity, empower you to make informed decisions about your money, future, and freedom. This book is a quick AI interactive guide summarizing open source YouTube videos from industry experts.

Thank you for investing your time into this knowledge. My hope is that it helps you build a stronger knowledge base, understand our changing world, and contribute meaningfully to a more open, fair, and abundant future.

To your freedom and prosperity,

-Dr. Randall G. Sampson

Disclaimer

This content is for informational and educational purposes only and should not be considered financial advice. Please conduct your own research and consult with a qualified financial advisor before making any investment decisions.

The Bitcoin Pocket Book

Copyright © 2025 by Liberty Leadership Development

All rights reserved. No part of this publication may be reproduced, distributed, or transmitted in any form or by any means, including photocopying, recording, or other electronic or mechanical methods, without the prior written permission of the publisher, except in the case of brief quotations embodied in critical reviews and certain other noncommercial uses permitted by copyright law.

Cover design by Liberty Leadership Development

Published by Liberty Leadership Development

Table of Contents

1. The Birth and Fundamentals of Bitcoin
2. Bitcoin Mining Explained
3. There Is No Second Best – Understanding Bitcoin's Uniqueness
4. What is Bitcoin, and Why is it Worth Anything?
5. 15 Essential Lessons for Accelerating Wealth with Bitcoin
6. The Paradigm Shift — Bitcoin's Rise as a Financial Cornerstone
7. The Coming Wave of US Money Printing & Its Impact on Bitcoin
8. There Is No Second Best — Understanding Bitcoin's Uniqueness (Jack Mallers Keynote)
9. The 21 Ways to Wealth — A Bitcoin-Centric Blueprint
10. Identifying Bitcoin Market Cycle Tops Using Key Indicators
11. Understanding Bitcoin's Price Cycles — Liquidity, Leverage, and Behavior
12. The 8% Rule, Bitcoin's Outperformance, and Workplace Mindset
13. The Transformative Role of Bitcoin in Human Civilization
14. Bitcoin & Blockchain — A Comprehensive Introduction
15. There Is No Second Best — Bitcoin's Singular Superiority
16. The Bitcoin Revolution — Rebuilding the Global Economy with Digital Capital
17. The Future of Bitcoin in Corporate Finance — Insights from Michael Saylor
18. Bitcoin Value, Supply & Demand — Insights from Bitwise CIO Matt Hogan
19. How Money and Banking Work — And Why They're Broken Today
20. Best Places to Buy Bitcoin in the USA (2025 Guide)
21. Bitcoin, Broken Money, and the Future of Economic Freedom

Chapter 1

The Birth and Fundamentals of Bitcoin

Overview

This summary outlines the origins, design, and significance of Bitcoin, a decentralized digital currency introduced in response to the 2008 financial crisis.

Background: Financial Crisis and Loss of Trust

In 2008, global banks' mismanagement led to a severe financial crisis. Many people lost their homes, and trust in traditional financial systems collapsed.

Introduction of Bitcoin

On October 31, 2008, an anonymous figure or group known as Satoshi Nakamoto published the Bitcoin white paper online. The paper proposed a peer-to-peer electronic cash system, enabling secure currency transfers without banks or third parties. The white paper was only nine pages and outlined a revolutionary, code-based, decentralized payment network.

Launch and Symbolic Origins

Bitcoin's network went live in January 2009. The first block (the "genesis block") included a Times newspaper headline: "Chancellor on the Brink of Second Bailout for Banks," highlighting the motivation for Bitcoin's creation.

How Bitcoin Works

Bitcoin is operated by thousands of computers (nodes) globally, not controlled by any single entity. Transactions are verified through a consensus mechanism, ensuring validity and preventing double-spending. The decentralized structure means no central point of failure; the network remains operational even if parts are attacked or go offline.

Bitcoin Creation and Distribution

There will only ever be 21 million Bitcoin, unlike fiat currencies that can be printed at will. New Bitcoin are distributed through mining: computers solve complex puzzles, and the first to solve each puzzle adds a new block to the blockchain and earns Bitcoin as a reward (block reward). This mining process secures and maintains the network. Every four years, the block reward halves—a process called "halving"—reducing new Bitcoin supply and historically increasing its price.

Significance and Uses

Bitcoin is decentralized, open to anyone with internet access, and not reliant on banks or governments. It serves as an investment, a store of value, a means for cross-border payments, and a hedge against currency devaluation.

Conclusion

Since 2009, Bitcoin has evolved from a digital currency into a multifaceted financial tool, representing a major shift in how money can be used and controlled.

The Birth and Fundamentals of Bitcoin

Watch the related video http://bit.ly/4nwciz5

Scan QR Code to watch video

Chapter 2

Bitcoin Mining Explained

Overview

This text provides a non-technical explanation of how bitcoins are created and the role of miners in the Bitcoin ecosystem. It covers the mining process, incentives, increasing difficulty, and collaborative mining solutions.

Bitcoin Creation

Bitcoins are not printed but "mined" using computers running special programs. There is a finite supply: a maximum of 21 million bitcoins can ever exist. Over 12 million bitcoins had been mined at the time of writing.

Mining Process

Miners solve complex mathematical problems to extract new bitcoins. Mining requires significant energy and computational power.

Role of Miners

Besides generating new bitcoins, miners verify transactions and help prevent fraud. More miners lead to faster transaction verification and reduced fraud.

Miner Compensation

Miners earn two types of rewards: newly generated bitcoins and transaction fees from the transactions they verify.

Mining Difficulty

To keep the Bitcoin creation rate steady, mining difficulty increases as more miners join. Early on, mining was easy (e.g., 200 bitcoins with a home computer in 2009). By 2014, mining a single bitcoin could take about 98 years on a standard computer.

Specialized Mining Hardware

ASIC miners (powerful, specialized computers) were developed to handle increased difficulty. Solo mining has become impractical due to competition.

Mining Pools

Miners join pools to combine resources and share rewards based on their contribution.

Bitcoin Mining Explained

Watch the related video http://bit.ly/45OyuOA

Scan QR Code to Watch Video

Chapter 3

There Is No Second Best – Understanding Bitcoin's Uniqueness

Overview

This keynote by Jack Mallers explores why Bitcoin is fundamentally different from altcoins, focusing on proof of work (PoW) as Bitcoin's defining feature that anchors it to physical reality. Mallers explores the philosophical, technical, and security implications of this distinction, arguing that only Bitcoin offers true digital scarcity and decentralized protection.

Understanding Proof of Work (PoW)

Physical vs. Abstract:

- Digital representations (files, folders, social media actions) are abstractions, not physical reality.
- PoW is the bridge that connects the digital world to the physical, making digital actions carry real-world costs.

Reification: People often mistake digital abstractions for reality (e.g., "the menu is not the meal").

Abstract Power vs. Physical Power:

- Abstract power (e.g., social media, fiat money) is efficient but unchecked, invisible, and trust-dependent.
- Physical power (e.g., military, gold) is tangible, verifiable, inclusive, but energy-intensive and risky.

The Invention of PoW and Its Importance

Adam Back's HashCash (1996): Introduced hash cost functions to impose real costs on digital actions (e.g., email spam).

Satoshi Nakamoto's Bitcoin (2009): Used PoW to secure a decentralized digital ledger, allowing anyone to participate by expending energy.

PoW as Reverse Reification: Converts physical energy into a digital proof, making it the only physically real thing on a digital screen.

Security: PoW ensures that updating the Bitcoin ledger requires real-world effort, making attacks costly and defense universally accessible.

Bitcoin vs. Altcoins

Proof of Work (Bitcoin) vs. Proof of Stake (Altcoins):

- PoW is grounded in physical laws; PoS creates a simulated universe with its own rules, detached from physical reality.
- PoS systems concentrate power among those with the most coins (proof of rank), making them vulnerable to takeover by wealthy actors (e.g., BlackRock).

Security and Fairness:

- PoW allows anyone to defend the network by expending energy; PoS relies on trusting large stakeholders.
- Altcoins often have pre-mined supplies, frequent rule changes, and centralized decision-making (e.g., Ethereum's DAO hack reversal).

Equitability: Bitcoin is open, decentralized, and fair; altcoins tend to centralize power and privilege insiders.

Philosophical and Practical Implications

Digital Gold vs. Digital App Store:

- Bitcoin is likened to digital gold—unchanging, secure, and a store of value.

- Ethereum and other altcoins are compared to growth stocks or platforms (e.g., Apple), focusing on financialization and tokenization.

Danger of False Equivalence: The altcoin industry promotes the idea that all cryptocurrencies are similar, but only Bitcoin offers true decentralization and security.

Key Points

- **Proof of Work vs. Proof of Stake**: PoW requires real-world energy expenditure, ensuring security and decentralization. PoS relies on stake ownership, leading to centralization risks.

- **Philosophical Implications**: PoW bridges the digital and physical worlds, making Bitcoin the only truly decentralized digital asset.

- **Altcoin Limitations**: Altcoins are likened to centralized platforms with pre-mined coins and frequent protocol changes, contrasting Bitcoin's rigid, predictable rules.

Conclusion

"There is no second best." Bitcoin stands alone as the only cryptocurrency fundamentally anchored in physical reality.

There Is No Second Best – Understanding Bitcoin's Uniqueness

Watch the related video http://bit.ly/4kpMuSu

Scan QR Code to View Video

Chapter 4

What is Bitcoin, and Why is it Worth Anything?

Overview

This chapter explains Bitcoin's origin, technology, unique features, and why people believe it has real monetary value. In 2008 after the Great Recession, which eroded trust in traditional banks and financial systems; the pseudonymous Satoshi Nakamoto launched a peer-to-peer digital currency operating without central authorities.

Bitcoin's Origins and Purpose

- Emerged in 2008 after the Great Recession exposed flaws in traditional banking.
- Created by the pseudonymous Satoshi Nakamoto.
- Purpose: a peer-to-peer currency without central authority.

How Bitcoin Works

- Built on blockchain: a public, tamper-resistant ledger.
- Decentralized network of nodes keeps it secure and transparent.
- Cryptography ensures that transactions can't be reversed or forged.
- Self-custody: users control their coins via private keys and wallets.

Unique Features and Value Proposition

- Capped supply: only 21 million coins can ever exist.

- Seen as "digital gold" — scarce, durable, portable.
- Gaining legitimacy: ETFs, national mining, sovereign reserves.
- Lindy effect: survived over 15 years, so its odds of enduring rise.

Why It Has Value

- Like fiat currency, value is based on shared belief and acceptance.
- High speculation and volatility echo gold's early history.
- Resilience despite skepticism proves its real-world staying power.

Conclusion

Bitcoin's worth comes from its technological design, scarcity, decentralization, and growing global trust.

What is Bitcoin, and Why is it Worth Anything?

Watch the related video http://bit.ly/3G75k2U

Scan QR Code To Watch Video

Chapter 5

15 Essential Lessons for Accelerating Wealth with Bitcoin

Overview

A practical guide for building long-term wealth with Bitcoin through mindset shifts, self-custody, tax awareness, and smart strategies.

1. Paradigm Shift

Bitcoin is a monetary revolution, not just a stock. Study the white paper to see how it rewires incentives. Treating it like a stock leads to missed opportunities.

2. Early Advantage

Early conviction pays. Start small if you're skeptical.

3. Core Stack

Have a portion you'll never sell; use another portion for potential profit-taking.

4. Adoption Curve

Think in decades. Bitcoin's adoption curve rewards patience; not for quick day trading

5. Halving Cycle

Historically, bitcoin's four-year halving cycles create predictable price swings.

6. Liquidity

Global liquidity drives price more than headlines. Monitor liquidity indicators (e.g., Fed balance sheet, Global M2).

7. Psychology

Understand market sentiment cycles to avoid panic. Study behavioral finance to recognize optimal times for buying or holding.

8. Community Conviction

Conviction grows through experience — join Bitcoin meetups and conferences to strengthen your knowledge base and network.

9. Time Preference

Bitcoin encourages delayed gratification. Journal how it changes your decisions.

10. Self-Custody

"Not your keys, not your coins." Always use a personal hardware wallet, also known as cold storage.

11. Spend Regret

Spending Bitcoin often brings regret later. Use fiat (dollars/cash) for expenses, save Bitcoin for wealth preservation; spend fiat first.

12. Holdover Trade

Long-term holding beats day trading for most people.

13. Sound Money

Study Austrian economics to grasp why Bitcoin matters.

14. Compliance

Plan for taxes. Borrowing against Bitcoin isn't taxable — selling is.

15. Personal Growth

Bitcoin rewards discipline and learning. Evolve with it.

Conclusion

Bitcoin is a tool for wealth and freedom — but only if you apply sound principles, patience, and discipline. Adopt a long-term mindset, and learning from the experience of others.

15 Essential Lessons for Accelerating Wealth with Bitcoin

Watch the related video http://bit.ly/3ZZWcUu

Scan QR Code To Watch Video

Chapter 6

The Paradigm Shift — Bitcoin's Rise as a Financial Cornerstone

Overview

How Bitcoin shifted from "risky speculation" to a critical portfolio component for protecting wealth against traditional system risks. There is a significant shift among investors, institutions, and thought leaders—framing Bitcoin not as a speculative asset but as an essential portfolio component and a hedge against the risks of traditional finance.

Changing Perceptions

- Bitcoin is increasingly seen as a "safe haven" asset, not just a speculative investment.
- Influential figures (e.g., Larry Fink of BlackRock, Mohamed El-Erian) now describe Bitcoin as critical for portfolio quality and risk management.
- BlackRock research suggests an ideal Bitcoin allocation of 85-110% in portfolios, signaling a radical shift in institutional attitudes.

The Overton Window

- The narrative has moved from "Bitcoin is risky" to "it's risky not to own Bitcoin."
- This shift is driven by growing awareness of systemic risks (debt, inflation, geopolitical instability) in traditional finance.

Smart Allocation

- Advocates suggest different allocation strategies based on wealth:
- Those with little to lose or much to spare may allocate nearly all their assets to Bitcoin.
- Middle-class investors might consider a balanced approach (e.g., 50%).
- Emphasis on understanding and comfort with Bitcoin before increasing exposure.

Systemic Risks
- Pensions and retirement systems are portrayed as increasingly unreliable due to rising retirement ages, decreasing life expectancy, and inflation eroding value.
- Self-directed IRAs in the US and similar structures elsewhere allow for Bitcoin exposure within retirement accounts, but options are limited in the UK and Europe.
- The suggestion is that relying solely on traditional pension systems may guarantee poverty in retirement.

Long-Term Outlook
- Over long timeframes, Bitcoin is expected to appreciate significantly, potentially outperforming traditional models and assumptions.
- Attempts to time the market or sell Bitcoin for short-term gains are discouraged; holding through volatility is recommended.

Closing Thoughts
The financial world is undergoing a fundamental transformation, with Bitcoin at its center. The question is not if, but how much Bitcoin will shape the future of wealth. Individuals are urged to critically assess the risks of traditional finance and consider Bitcoin as a means of protecting and growing wealth for themselves and their families.

The Paradigm Shift — Bitcoin's Rise as a Financial Cornerstone

Watch the related video http://bit.ly/3TZCOmM

Scan QR Code To Watch Video

Chapter 7

The Coming Wave of US Money Printing & Its Impact on Bitcoin

Overview

A forecast on why new money printing is inevitable — and how it could push Bitcoin to $1 million. This content is focused on US government money printing, its implications for markets—especially Bitcoin—and the mechanisms likely to drive a new era of liquidity and inflation. The chapter critiques the bond market, outlines why government borrowing is unsustainable without further intervention, and predicts a massive increase in money supply by 2028, with Bitcoin as a primary beneficiary.

Background

Since 2017, US debt soared 80%. Bonds underperformed stocks, gold, and Bitcoin badly.

Bond Market Crisis

Bonds can't compete with riskier assets. Selling more debt won't work without heavy money printing.

- **Poor Returns:** Bonds have dramatically underperformed compared to NASDAQ, gold, and Bitcoin (up to 99% underperformance vs. Bitcoin).
- **Difficulty Selling Bonds:** The US needs to sell increasing amounts of debt, but investors get better returns elsewhere, creating a funding challenge for the government.

Government's Response

Deficits keep climbing. The solution? Create more liquidity (print more money) to inflate Gross Domestic Product (GDP).

- **Deficit Trends:** Despite political rhetoric about spending cuts, US deficits are hitting new records, with little real action to reduce them.
- **Growth Focus:** Policymakers are emphasizing nominal GDP growth as a solution, which effectively means increasing credit and money supply.

Mechanisms for Money Printing and Market Impact

Financial Bubble Creation: Authorities may encourage new bubbles (e.g., in crypto) or boost lending to the real economy ("QE for poor people") to stimulate growth.

Inflation as a Tool: Inflation is seen as necessary to manage the debt burden, making assets like Bitcoin attractive as hedges.

How This Unfolds

1. Tax foreign bond holders to boost local demand.

2. Loosen banking leverage rules so banks buy more Treasuries.

3. Release Fannie Mae & Freddie Mac to inject trillions via mortgages.

Three-Pronged Path to $1 Million Bitcoin

1. Capital Controls vs. Tariffs:

- Likely move to tax foreign holders of US debt, especially short-term instruments, to encourage long-term bond demand and control the yield curve.
- This could raise over $1 trillion but risks losing foreign investment, necessitating even more domestic money creation.

2. Bank Supplemental Leverage Ratio (SLR) Exemption:

- Removing SLR restrictions would let banks buy Treasuries with effectively infinite leverage, boosting their profits and supporting bond demand.
- US banks could also issue stablecoins, collecting deposits at no yield and investing in Treasuries for risk-free profit.

3. Fannie Mae and Freddie Mac Liquidity Injection:

- Ending conservatorship would allow these entities to issue massive amounts of mortgage debt, injecting up to $5 trillion into markets.

Quantitative Projections and Bitcoin Implications

Estimated Money Creation: Between now and 2028, up to $9 trillion could be injected into the US economy via bank credit, bond purchases, and mortgage liquidity.

Comparison to COVID Stimulus: COVID-era stimulus was ~$4 trillion, which drove Bitcoin up 10x; the coming wave is projected to be double that.

Bitcoin Price Target: With increased liquidity and less Bitcoin available on exchanges, a $1 million Bitcoin price is deemed plausible.

Conclusion

If new stimulus hits, Bitcoin could surge to $1 million. Bonds look unattractive; Bitcoin is the hedge.

The Coming Wave of US Money Printing & Its Impact on Bitcoin

Watch the related video http://bit.ly/45OR5dp

Scan QR Code To Watch Video

Chapter 8

There Is No Second Best — Understanding Bitcoin's Uniqueness

Overview

A keynote by Jack Mallers arguing Bitcoin is fundamentally different from all altcoins due to its use of proof of work (PoW).

Core Thesis

"**There is no second best.**" Only Bitcoin uses energy (PoW) to tie digital value to the physical world.

Proof of Work vs. Proof of Stake

- PoW converts physical energy into secure digital money.

- PoS systems (Ethereum, altcoins) create digital simulations without grounding in physical laws.

- PoS concentrates power among the wealthiest holders, making them prone to centralization.

Security Implications

- PoW ensures updating Bitcoin's ledger requires real-world effort, making attacks costly.

- PoS depends on trusting stakeholders rather than expending energy.

Philosophical Takeaways

- Bitcoin is digital gold: scarce, secure, unchanging.
- Altcoins are like digital app platforms: dynamic but centralized and mutable.

Conclusion

Only Bitcoin combines physical security with digital scarcity, making it uniquely decentralized and resistant to manipulation.

There Is No Second Best — Understanding Bitcoin's Uniqueness

Watch the related video http://bit.ly/45YWpep

Scan QR Code To Watch Video

Chapter 9

The 21 Ways to Wealth — A Bitcoin-Centric Blueprint

Overview

A motivational framework outlining **21 principles** to build generational wealth centered on Bitcoin. This chapter positions Bitcoin as superior to traditional assets, advocating for its adoption alongside leveraging technology, legal structures, and personal virtues to maximize generational wealth.

Bitcoin as Perfected Capital

- Bitcoin is described as "perfected, programmable, incorruptible capital" with engineered superiority over gold, real estate, equities, and other assets.
- This chapter predicts Bitcoin will appreciate faster than all other assets and urges individuals and families to allocate capital into Bitcoin for long-term prosperity.

Key Principles

1. **Clarity** – Recognize Bitcoin as perfected capital.

2. **Conviction** – Believe in its engineered superiority.

3. **Courage** – Take intelligent monetary risks.

4. **Cooperation** – Align family and generational resources.

5. **Capability** – Master AI to accelerate knowledge.

6. **Composition** – Structure strong legal and asset protections.

7. **Citizenship** – Choose freedom-respecting jurisdictions.

8. **Civility** – Respect social and political contexts.

9. **Corporation** – Leverage corporate structures for growth.

10. **Focus** – Concentrate on the highest probability strategy (Bitcoin).

11. **Equity** – Share upside to accelerate wealth.

12. **Credit** – Use debt instruments strategically.

13. **Compliance** – Operate within legal frameworks for efficiencies.

14. **Capitalization** – Raise and reinvest relentlessly.

15. **Communication** – Build trust through transparency.

16. **Commitment** – Maintain focus on Bitcoin.

17. **Consistency** – Execute reliably for market leadership.

18. **Adaptation** – Prepare for inevitable change.

19. **Evolution** – Build sustainably, avoiding overextension.

20. **Advocacy** – Inspire and educate others.

21. **Generosity** – Share success to create lasting impact.

Closing Message

"It might make sense to get some [Bitcoin] in case it catches on." Build wealth with clarity, courage, and disciplined focus on Bitcoin.

The 21 Ways to Wealth — A Bitcoin-Centric Blueprint

Watch the related video http://bit.ly/4ev1QUq

Scan QR Code To Watch Video

Chapter 10

Identifying Bitcoin Market Cycle Tops Using Key Indicators

Overview

Bitcoin's price is surging, raising questions about how much higher it can go and when to stop buying. Historical bull runs end with euphoria and sharp corrections, so timing exits is crucial to avoid losses. How to use data-driven indicators to avoid buying at market tops.

Five Key Indicators

1. **MVRV Z-Score**

    - Compares market value to realized value.

    - Red zone historically signals cycle tops.

2. **NUPL**

    - Tracks unrealized profits/losses to gauge market euphoria.

3. **Pi Cycle Top Indicator**

    - Moving average crossovers pinpoint tops within days.

4. **Puell Multiple**

    - Miner revenue vs. historical average; high values indicate selling pressure.

5. **Bitcoin Rainbow Chart**

- Logarithmic regression shows long-term valuation bands.

Current Status (June 2025)

None are in danger zones yet, but all are rising, suggesting a strong bull phase with caution needed.

Pro Tip

Avoid trying to time exact tops. While Bitcoin is in a strong bull market, key indicators suggest it has not yet reached a cycle top, but caution is warranted as they approach warning levels. Investors should use a combination of data-driven tools, avoid emotional decisions, and focus on long-term accumulation

Identifying Bitcoin Market Cycle Tops Using Key Indicators

Watch the related video http://bit.ly/44KNrjA

Scan QR Code To Watch Video

Chapter 11

Understanding Bitcoin's Price Cycles — Liquidity, Leverage, and Behavior

Overview

Explains **three fundamental drivers** of Bitcoin's price movements.

1. Global Liquidity (GLI)

- Fuel for price rises; Bitcoin acts as a barometer for global liquidity changes.

2. Leverage (DRS)

- The accelerator or brake; current leverage is low, suggesting room for growth.

3. Network Profitability (NPRS)

- Tracks how many holders are in profit or loss, influencing sentiment and potential selling.

Combined Signal
- Combining these three indicators (GRS, DRS, NPRS) shows the market is in a neutral to slightly bullish phase, with historical data suggesting strong odds of further price appreciation over the next 30-180 days.
- The presented framework is not a tool for predicting exact tops or bottoms but helps identify when Bitcoin is overbought or oversold, guiding strategic positioning rather than market timing.
- The speaker advises against trying to time the market, recommending conviction-weighted and tiered entries based on risk levels, and highlights the importance of dynamic risk assessment as market conditions evolve.

Conclusion

Bitcoin's price cycles are not random but are governed by identifiable, data-driven factors: liquidity, leverage, and investor psychology. By monitoring these key indicators, investors can better position themselves for long-term success, focusing on risk-adjusted strategies rather than attempting to predict short-term price movements.

Understanding Bitcoin's Price Cycles — Liquidity, Leverage, and Behavior

Watch the related video http://bit.ly/45UkeDZ

Scan QR Code To Watch Video

Chapter 12

The 8% Rule, Bitcoin's Outperformance, and Workplace Mindset

Overview
This content is a commentary and analysis session, hosted by Anthony Pompliano, covering three main topics: the significance of the 8% growth rate in finance, the evolving relationship between major banks and Bitcoin, and a viral reaction from Gary Vaynerchuk on workplace entitlement and remote work culture.

The 8% Rule

- Money supply and debt grow ~8% yearly.
- S&P 500 matches this growth, meaning real returns are minimal after inflation and taxes.

Bitcoin vs. Traditional Assets

- Bitcoin's CAGR: ~85% over 10 years, far outpacing fiat-denominated assets.

Banks Embracing Bitcoin

- JP Morgan and others now offer Bitcoin-backed loans and crypto ETFs, marking mainstream acceptance.

Workplace Entitlement

- Gary Vaynerchuk critiques remote work entitlement, emphasizing adaptability and competition in career growth.

Conclusion

Understand where old and new financial systems intersect. Adapt in finance and workplace mindset to thrive. The intersection of new (crypto) and old (traditional finance) worlds presents both risks and opportunities. Understand where these worlds meet to maximize returns and protect assets. In the workplace, adaptability and hard work are timeless values for success.

The 8% Rule, Bitcoin's Outperformance, and Workplace Mindset

Watch the related video http://bit.ly/4ldqvQ4

Scan QR Code To Watch Video

Chapter 13

The Transformative Role of Bitcoin in Human Civilization

Overview

A narrative exploring Bitcoin's historical context, invention, and imagined future impact.

Key Points

- **Post-WWII (1948):** Recovery amid devastation.

- **2008 Financial Crisis:** Banks fail, governments print money and fairness erode.

- **Bitcoin's Invention (2009):** Created as incorruptible money to protect individuals from monetary debasement.

- **2021 Reality:** Growing tyranny, division, and economic manipulation. Bitcoin gains traction as a tool for financial freedom.

- **2048 Vision:** Widespread Bitcoin adoption leads to prosperity—individualized education, clean energy, abundant food, and cultural renaissance.

- **2109 Future:** Bitcoin ends monetary tyranny, enabling global harmony, creativity, and health.

Conclusion

Bitcoin is presented as a revolutionary technology that protects wealth, enables freedom, and prevents the cycles of tyranny and economic collapse, ultimately ushering in a new era of prosperity, creativity, and stability for future generations.

The Transformative Role of Bitcoin in Human Civilization

Watch the related video http://bit.ly/44Npb0k

Scan QR Code To Watch Video

Chapter 14

Bitcoin & Blockchain — A Comprehensive Introduction

Overview

An accessible explanation of Bitcoin, blockchain, and the evolution of the Internet (Web 1, 2, and 3).

Key Points

- **What is Bitcoin?**

    - **Function:** Enables sending and receiving value globally using only a computer and internet connection, without needing a trusted middleman.
    - **Definition:** Bitcoin is the world's first cryptocurrency, operating on the first public blockchain network.
    - **Revolutionary Aspect:** Bitcoin is the first public digital payments infrastructure, open to all and not owned by any single entity.

- **Significance**

    - **Global Reach:** Bitcoin is the first globally accessible public money.
    - **Public Infrastructure:** Unlike traditional digital payments (which rely on private banks), Bitcoin's ledger is public and accessible to anyone.
    - **Accessibility:** Anyone, regardless of background or credit, can create a Bitcoin address for free to receive digital payments.

- **Imperfections**

    - **Historical Comparison:** Like early email, Bitcoin is a work in progress but marks a significant breakthrough in computer science.

- **Not Perfect:** Bitcoin is not universally accepted, not commonly used for pricing, and its value can be unstable.

- **Need for Decentralization**

  - **Risks of Centralization:** Current private infrastructure (banks, corporations) is vulnerable to large-scale hacks and failures (e.g., Equifax breach, SWIFT hacks, IoT vulnerabilities).
  - **Single Points of Failure:** Centralized systems create vulnerabilities; decentralization removes these choke points, similar to how the Internet democratized communications.

- **Blockchain Beyond Bitcoin**

  - **Public Infrastructure:** Unlike traditional digital payments (which rely on private banks), Bitcoin's ledger is public and accessible to anyone.
  - **Accessibility:** Anyone, regardless of background or credit, can create a Bitcoin address for free to receive digital payments.
  - **Global Reach:** Bitcoin is the first globally accessible public money.

- **Internet Evolution**

  - **Web 1:** Read-only, curated content (e.g., AOL).
  - **Web 2:** Interactive, user-generated content, but centralized and monetized by a few large companies (e.g., Facebook, Google).
  - **Web 3:** Decentralized ownership of networks through crypto assets (tokens), allowing users to own and govern the underlying infrastructure.

Conclusion

Blockchain and crypto represent a shift towards user-owned, censorship-resistant infrastructure.

Bitcoin & Blockchain — A Comprehensive Introduction

Watch the related video http://bit.ly/4nxS4Vy

Scan QR Code To Watch Video

Chapter 15

There Is No Second Best — Bitcoin's Singular Superiority

Overview

A persuasive presentation arguing Bitcoin is the only viable choice as digital capital. This chapter is a comprehensive, persuasive presentation on why Bitcoin is the singular, superior digital asset. The details systematically compares Bitcoin to other assets (digital and physical), arguing that Bitcoin is not only the best in its class but that, in each relevant category, "there is no second best." The talk covers digital transformation, Bitcoin's technical and economic properties, its societal impact, and its unique position as an investment, commodity, property, and capital asset.

Key Points

- **Digital Transformation**
    - Bitcoin is the digital transformation of money and capital, converting energy into secure digital property.

- **Market Dominance**
    - Represents 97% of proof-of-work crypto market cap.

- **Institutional Acceptance**
    - Bitcoin is treated as a commodity, unlike other cryptos facing regulatory barriers.

- **Superiority Over Commodities & Property**

- Bitcoin is the first absolutely scarce asset—more scarce than gold or land.

- **Treasury and Capital Asset**

  - Bitcoin outpaces inflation and preserves shareholder value unlike cash or bonds.

- **Alternative Investment**

  - Uncorrelated to traditional assets, making it a strategic allocation.

Bitcoin as Digital Capital

Only 0.1% of global capital is currently digital; Bitcoin leads this nascent transformation. Bitcoin, via crypto proof-of-work, uniquely converts energy into secure, transferable digital capital. Proof-of-work ensures Bitcoin's decentralization, security, and physical linkage to the real world.

Bitcoin's Unique Superiority

- **Market Dominance:** Bitcoin represents 97% of proof-of-work crypto market cap; no other crypto asset comes close.
- **Institutional Acceptance:** Only Bitcoin is accepted as a commodity, not a security; other cryptos face regulatory barriers and lack mainstream adoption.
- **Network Security:** Bitcoin is protected by the world's most powerful computer network, using vast, globally distributed energy resources.
- **Decentralization:** Mining seeks out cheap, stranded energy worldwide, making centralization impossible.

Brand, Adoption, and Investment

- **Global Brand:** 220 million holders; 420 million crypto users. Bitcoin is the universal crypto brand, accepted everywhere.

- **Investment Brand:** Bitcoin is the most widely held and recognized investment asset globally, transcending national currencies and physical assets.
- **Standardization:** Like Standard Oil in energy, Bitcoin is the standard for capital—open, global, and accessible to all.

Bitcoin vs. Commodities and Property

- **Digital Commodity:** Bitcoin is the only truly digital, fixed-supply commodity, superior to gold and all physical commodities.
- **Scarcity:** Bitcoin is the first absolutely scarce asset—more comparable to time than to any physical commodity or land.
- **Digital Property:** Bitcoin is the best property—global, divisible, immortal, immune to political risk, and accessible to all, unlike physical real estate.

Capital Asset and Treasury Use

- **Pure Economic Energy:** Bitcoin is the first asset representing pure, immortal, indestructible economic energy.
- **Beating Inflation:** Bitcoin is the only asset that outpaces the cost of capital and inflation; all others are dilutive.
- **Treasury Asset:** Holding Bitcoin as a treasury asset is accretive, unlike cash or bonds, which dilute shareholder value.

The Best Tech and Alternative Investment

- **Tech Investment:** Like early investments in Apple or Amazon, Bitcoin is an unstoppable, misunderstood technology that will yield outsized returns as adoption grows.
- **Alternative Asset:** Bitcoin is uncorrelated to currencies, corporations, or counterparties, making it the best alternative investment for family offices and institutions.

Bitcoin as a New Asset Class and Ecosystem

- **Ecosystem Growth:** Bitcoin underpins a growing ecosystem of securities, ETFs, corporate treasuries, and financial products worldwide.
- **Capital Ratchet:** Bitcoin's adoption and leverage only increase; its network effect is self-reinforcing.

Societal Impact

- **Best Bank:** Bitcoin serves as a global, egalitarian savings account, free from corporate or national agendas.
- **Path to Peace and Prosperity:** As an open, transparent, decentralized network, Bitcoin offers a fair way to settle global differences and empower all economic classes.

Evolution and Outlook

- **Adoption Phases:** Bitcoin has moved from the era of idealists (2008–2020), through the crazy years (2020–2024), into institutional adoption (2024+), with growth from $0 to $1.4 trillion and aiming for $100 trillion.
- **Unstoppable Idea:** Bitcoin, as the best idea, channels scarce time and energy into the most powerful form of economic energy.

Conclusion

In every category—digital capital, commodity, property, treasury, banking—Bitcoin is the singular choice. Bitcoin is not just the best, but the only real choice.Study, buy, hold, build on, advocate for, defend, and enjoy Bitcoin.Bitcoin is the best idea of our time; its moment has arrived, and no force can stop it. There is no second best.

There Is No Second Best — Bitcoin's Singular Superiority

Watch the related video http://bit.ly/3IukPSY

Scan QR Code To Watch Video

Chapter 16

The Bitcoin Revolution — Rebuilding the Global Economy with Digital Capital

Overview

A keynote outlining how Bitcoin transforms capital preservation for individuals, corporations, and nations.focusing on the transformative potential of Bitcoin as a form of "digital capital." The speaker contrasts outdated 20th-century financial systems with Bitcoin's promise for the 21st century, offering strategic advice for individuals, corporations, institutions, and nations on adopting Bitcoin to preserve and grow wealth. The presentation includes historical analogies, asset comparisons, and future forecasts.

The Problem with Traditional Assets

Outdated Systems: The global economy relies on slow, expensive, and inefficient 20th-century financial systems (e.g., limited trading hours, high friction).

Capital Preservation Challenges: Both financial (stocks, bonds, fiat currencies) and physical assets (real estate, gold, art) are eroded by inflation, taxes, maintenance, and other risks.

Useful Life of Assets: Most financial assets last ~30 years; physical assets, 50–75 years at best, due to entropy and external threats.

Bitcoin as Digital Capital

Unique Properties: Bitcoin is described as immortal, immutable, immaterial, and with an infinite lifespan—immune to many risks facing traditional assets.

Preservation Efficiency: Custodied Bitcoin can last 1,000 years; self-custodied, 10,000 years; AI-managed, 100,000 years.

Superior Store of Value: Compared to other assets, Bitcoin offers unparalleled longevity and resilience.

Strategic Asset Allocation

- **Trade Up the Ladder:** Move from fragile, depreciating assets (e.g., fiat, physical goods) to resilient, scarce, and digital assets (Bitcoin).
- **Historical Parallels:** Analogies to the Dutch purchase of Manhattan, Louisiana Purchase, and Alaska Purchase illustrate the outsized returns from visionary asset swaps.

Bitcoin's Growth and Forecast

- **Current and Future Value:** Bitcoin is currently a tiny fraction (~0.1%) of global wealth but is forecasted to rise significantly (potentially $13M per coin by 2045).
- **Performance:** Bitcoin has delivered 55% annual returns over four years, vastly outperforming bonds.
- **Individual, Corporate, and Institutional Strategies**
- **Individuals:** Strategies range from conservative ("normie") to aggressive ("triple maxie") with increasing Bitcoin allocations and leverage, showing exponential wealth outcomes.
- **Corporations:** Convert capital and cash flows to Bitcoin, issue debt/equity to acquire more, and avoid dilutive practices. MicroStrategy is cited as a successful example.
- **Institutions:** Endowments and nonprofits are advised to shift from short-duration assets to long-duration (Bitcoin), using leverage wisely.

National Strategies

- **Indebted Nations:** Reallocate reserves (from gold/bonds) to Bitcoin; issue currency or debt to acquire Bitcoin, with first movers gaining the most.
- **Wealthy Nations:** Allocate significant surpluses to Bitcoin for financial and national security, but note limited room for "triple maxie" adoption at the nation-state level.

- **US Case:** Adoption of Bitcoin can address half of the nation's financial challenges, while technology and AI-driven growth address the rest.

The Future of Capital

Digital Migration: Capital will flow from underperforming physical and financial assets into Bitcoin, "demonetizing" less efficient stores of value globally

---

Key Points

- **Traditional Assets Limitations**

    - Physical and financial assets decay or are eroded by inflation and risk.

- **Bitcoin as Digital Capital**

    - Immortal, immutable, with an infinite lifespan if securely held.

- **Strategic Asset Allocation**

    - Move from fragile assets to resilient Bitcoin for outsized returns.

- **Forecast**

    - Potential for Bitcoin to reach ~$13M per coin by 2045.

- **Strategies for Individuals & Organizations**

    - Individuals: Gradual to aggressive Bitcoin allocation.

    - Corporations: Convert capital flows to Bitcoin, raise debt or equity to acquire more.

    - Institutions: Shift endowment funds from short-duration to Bitcoin.

- **National Strategy**

- First-mover nations gain the most by reallocating reserves to Bitcoin.

Conclusion

Bitcoin is positioned as the inevitable future of capital and money, offering individuals, organizations, and nations a path to preserve and grow wealth in the digital age. Strategic adoption and early action are emphasized as keys to benefiting from the ongoing Bitcoin revolution.

The Bitcoin Revolution — Rebuilding the Global Economy with Digital Capital

Watch the related video http://bit.ly/4kxf4Sc

Scan QR Code To Watch The Video

Chapter 17

The Future of Bitcoin in Corporate Finance — Insights from Michael Saylor

Overview

An interview with Michael Saylor the focus is on Bitcoin's transformative role in corporate finance, investment strategies, and macroeconomic resilience. The conversation covers the adoption of Bitcoin by corporations, new Bitcoin-backed financial products, macroeconomic uncertainties, and the evolving perception of Bitcoin among investors and governments.

Bitcoin's role in corporate strategy and macroeconomic resilience.

Bitcoin as a Corporate Treasury Asset

- ☐ **Adoption Trend:** Increasing interest from lesser-known and struggling companies in adopting Bitcoin as a treasury asset, with large corporations expected to follow later.
- ☐ **Rationale:** Companies outside the major tech giants are seeking new ways to regain relevance and financial strength, finding hope in Bitcoin's potential for digital transformation.
- ☐ **Performance:** Early adopters like MicroStrategy (now Strategy) and MetaPlanet have seen significant success, influencing others.

Traditional Finance vs. Bitcoin Standard

- ☐ **Conventional Playbook:** Historically, companies used cash reserves in treasury bills, buybacks, or dividends, but these strategies are seen as "decapitalizing."
- ☐ **Bitcoin's Role:** Bitcoin is positioned as the 21st-century reserve asset, offering superior returns and acting as a "shock absorber" during economic uncertainty.

- ☐ **Advantages:** Bitcoin is immune to tariffs, supply chain issues, and many risks associated with traditional finance and global operations.

Investment Strategies for Individuals

- ☐ **Long-Term Vision:** Saylor predicts a single Bitcoin could be worth $13 million by 2045, urging individuals to prioritize Bitcoin over luxury spending.
- ☐ **Practical Advice:** Keep your job, avoid unnecessary luxury purchases, use long-term mortgage debt as intelligent leverage, and invest in Bitcoin rather than paying off low-interest debt.

Macro Environment and Bitcoin's Resilience

- ☐ **Global Uncertainty:** Trade wars, sovereign debt issues, and macroeconomic instability create uncertainty, making Bitcoin more attractive as a safe haven.
- ☐ **Market Dynamics:** During crises, Bitcoin's liquidity and global tradability cause short-term volatility but long-term decoupling and upward rallies.
- ☐ **Investor Behavior:** Each crisis recruits new Bitcoin believers as traditional assets show vulnerabilities.

Innovative Bitcoin-Backed Financial Products

- ☐ **New Offerings:** Introduction of Strife (over-collateralized preferred stock with a 10% perpetual dividend) and Strike (8% coupon, partial upside, principal protection) to suit different investor risk profiles.
- ☐ **Potential for Bitcoin Bonds:** Saylor supports the idea of government-issued Bitcoin-backed bonds, citing Bitcoin's high performance as a financial "universal sweetener."

Government and Institutional Adoption

- ☐ **US Government:** Surprised by recent rapid positive shifts in US government attitudes, including a strategic Bitcoin reserve and cabinet-level enthusiasm.
- ☐ **Adoption Pace:** Smaller, agile companies and nations are expected to move faster than large governments.

Market Rotation and Price Dynamics

- ☐ **Current Market:** Rotation from non-committed holders (e.g., bankruptcy trustees) to new, long-term investors via ETFs and treasury companies.
- ☐ **Price Movements:** Despite positive developments, price lags due to this rotation but is expected to rise as new investors enter.

Media and Mainstream Understanding

- ☐ **Exponential Adoption:** Mainstream media is slow to recognize Bitcoin's impact, but investor understanding is growing rapidly, likened to an exponential growth curve.
- ☐ **Investor Focus:** Investors are increasingly drawn to Bitcoin and Bitcoin treasury companies for their risk mitigation and superior returns.

Key Points

- **Bitcoin as Treasury Asset**
  - Early adopters like MicroStrategy outperform traditional treasury approaches.

- **Advantages Over Conventional Finance**
  - Immunity to supply chain disruptions, tariffs, and political risks.

- **Investment Advice**

- Prioritize Bitcoin accumulation over luxury spending; leverage mortgage debt intelligently.

- **New Bitcoin-Backed Financial Products**

  - Strife (10% dividend preferred stock) and Strike (8% coupon with partial upside) as innovative options.

- **Government Adoption Trends**

  - Smaller nations and companies will adopt before large governments.

- **Market Rotation**

  - From non-committed holders to long-term institutional investors via ETFs and treasuries.

Conclusion

Bitcoin is the ultimate corporate treasury asset, offering unparalleled protection and upside in an uncertain macro environment. People buy Bitcoin because they want to keep their money. Every crisis recruits a new class of Bitcoin believers.

The Future of Bitcoin in Corporate Finance — Insights from Michael Saylor

Watch the related video http://bit.ly/3GqOFax

Scan QR Code To Watch Video

Chapter 18

Bitcoin Value, Supply & Demand — Insights from Bitwise CIO Matt Hogan

Overview

The chapter is aimed at investors and crypto enthusiasts, covers why Bitcoin has value, how its price is determined, current market dynamics, comparisons to gold, institutional adoption, and addresses common questions about Bitcoin and other cryptocurrencies.

Why Does Bitcoin Have Value?

Service Provided: Bitcoin's core value is as a service—allowing wealth storage digitally without reliance on banks or governments.

Comparison to Other Services: Like Microsoft provides productivity tools, Bitcoin provides digital, bankless wealth storage. Demand for this service drives its price.

No Cash Flow: Unlike traditional investments, Bitcoin doesn't generate cash flow, but its utility as a service justifies its value.

Price Determination & Volatility

Supply and Demand: The price is set by market supply and demand, not by cash flows or traditional valuation models.

Volatility Context: Bitcoin's volatility is often criticized, but gold has also experienced significant drawdowns historically. Over long periods, Bitcoin has outperformed, especially post-COVID.

Current Market Dynamics

Supply Constraints: Only 164,000 new Bitcoin will be produced in 2024, enforced by the Bitcoin protocol.

Demand Drivers:

- **ETFs:** Bitcoin ETFs launched in January 2024, becoming the most successful ETF launch ever, with inflows far exceeding new supply.
- **Corporations:** Over 90 public companies (e.g., MicroStrategy, Tesla) hold Bitcoin, buying more than the annual new supply.
- **Governments:** A dozen+ governments now hold Bitcoin, including the US, which owns nearly 200,000 BTC. Bitwise predicts more countries will follow.
- **Structural Imbalance:** Demand from ETFs, corporations, and governments consistently exceeds new supply, forcing price increases as sellers become scarce.

Price Trends & Predictions

Behavioral Selling: Price stalls at round numbers (e.g., $72K, $100K) due to psychological resistance, then surges when these levels are breached.

Bitwise Prediction: Bitcoin could reach $200,000 by 2025 year-end if current demand trends persist.

De-risking of Bitcoin

- **Reduced Risks:** Early risks (technology, custody, regulation) have diminished. Major institutions and universities now hold Bitcoin, and custody solutions (e.g., Fidelity, Coinbase Custody) are robust.
- **Access:** Investors can buy Bitcoin via ETFs or self-custody; exchanges are riskier for larger holdings.

Other Cryptocurrencies (Ethereum, Solana, etc.)

Different Use Cases: Bitcoin is optimized for wealth storage ("digital gold"). Ethereum enables programmable money and decentralized applications. Other assets compete for niche roles.

Multiple Winners Likely: The crypto ecosystem may see several successful platforms serving different purposes.

Bitcoin Custody Options

Three Methods:

1. Self-custody (hardware wallet)
2. Exchange custody
3. ETF custody.

Best Practices: Self-custody or ETF (Coinbase Custody) are safest; exchange wallets are risky for significant amounts.

Price Movement Patterns

"Air Gaps": Expect price to move in jumps as psychological resistance levels are cleared, due to behavior-driven selling.

Bitcoin Network Security Post-Mining

Transaction Fees: When mining rewards end (~2140), transaction fees ("tips") will incentivize miners to maintain the network.

Regulation Impact

Positive Outlook: Regulation is advancing and expected to boost institutional adoption. Regulatory clarity is seen as a major catalyst for further inflows.

Bitcoin vs. Gold in Extreme Scenarios

Internet Outages: Bitcoin is inaccessible during global internet outages, but remains secure and accessible once connectivity returns. Gold remains a useful hedge.

Key Points

- **Core Value Proposition**

    - Bitcoin provides digital, bankless wealth storage.

- **Price Drivers**

    - Limited supply (21 million cap) vs. growing demand from ETFs, corporations, and governments.

- **Current Market Dynamics**

    - Demand exceeds new supply, pushing prices higher.

- **Price Patterns**

    - "Air gaps" occur when psychological resistance levels are breached.

- **Custody Options**

    - Self-custody, ETFs, or exchanges—with ETFs and hardware wallets being safest for large holdings.

- **Outlook**

    - Bitcoin is de-risked compared to early-years; regulatory clarity and institutional adoption fuel future growth.

Conclusion

Bitcoin's value arises from its unique service as digital, bankless wealth storage. Its price is driven by a structural mismatch between limited new supply and surging institutional, corporate, and governmental demand. The market has matured and de-risked, with robust custody solutions and growing regulatory clarity. While volatility and technical risks persist, the long-term outlook remains bullish if current trends continue. Other crypto assets serve different purposes, and the ecosystem is likely to have multiple winners.

Bitcoin Value, Supply & Demand — Insights from Bitwise CIO Matt Hogan

Watch the related video http://bit.ly/4nuErXc

Scan QR Code To Watch Video

Chapter 19

How Money and Banking Work — And Why They're Broken Today

Overview

A historical and systemic analysis by Lyn Alden of modern money and banking's flaws. In this educational explainer Lyn Alden summarizes the history, mechanics, and systemic problems of money and banking. It discusses the evolution from barter and commodity money to modern fiat systems, the rise of central banking, the causes and consequences of inflation and currency instability, and the emergence of decentralized alternatives like Bitcoin. The narrative connects historical developments to current issues, arguing that today's centralized, inflationary monetary systems are fundamentally flawed and exploring how open-source, decentralized money could offer solutions.

The Nature and Evolution of Money

- ☐ **Barter Limitations:** Barter is inefficient due to the difficulty of matching needs; as economies grow, trading pairs multiply rapidly.
- ☐ **Social Credit & Formal Credit:** Informal social credit evolves into formalized systems, with local authorities setting rules for credit and repayment.
- ☐ **Commodity Money:** Portable, durable, and scarce items (e.g., shell beads, gold, silver) become universal mediums of exchange.
- ☐ **Coins:** Gold and silver coins dominate due to scarcity, standardization, and regional acceptance.
- ☐ **Money as a Ledger:** Money records payments and savings, either governed by natural laws (commodity money) or by human agreements (credit).

The Rise of Banking and Centralization

- ☐ **Early Banking:** Systems like the Middle Eastern Suftaja and Hawala enabled safe, long-distance transfers based on trust and credit.
- ☐ **European Innovations:** Double-entry bookkeeping and negotiable paper instruments led to complex credit systems and financial institutions.
- ☐ **Fractional Reserve Banking:** Banks lend out more than they hold in reserves, creating systemic risk and periodic crises.
- ☐ **Central Banks:** Created to stabilize the system, central banks also enable governments to print money, leading to inflation and the eventual abandonment of gold standards.

The Modern Global Financial System

Three Eras:

1. International Gold Standard (1871–WWI): Centralized clearinghouses and telegraph communication increase efficiency but also risk.

2. Bretton Woods System (WWII–1971): U.S. dollar pegged to gold, other currencies pegged to the dollar; system collapses due to over-issuance of dollars.

3. Fiat and Petrodollar System (1971–present): Unbacked currencies, U.S. dollar as global reserve, and oil trade denominated in dollars.

Centralization and Abstraction: Power consolidates in central banks, ledgers become increasingly detached from physical assets, and states control currency issuance.

Systemic Problems and Consequences

- ☐ **Inflation and Currency Failure:** Most currencies lose value over time; hyperinflation and devaluation are common in developing countries.
- ☐ **Wealth Concentration:** Even in wealthy nations, money increasingly accumulates among elites, and public debt soars.
- ☐ **Incentive Problems:** The system enables subtle value extraction from the public, often benefiting insiders or corrupt officials.

- ☐ **Limited Upward Mobility:** Currency instability traps developing countries in cycles of dependence and inflation.

The Digital Age and Decentralized Alternatives

- ☐ **Bitcoin and Cryptography:** Bitcoin, launched in 2009, is the first decentralized digital currency enabling secure, borderless, and censorship-resistant transactions with a fixed supply.
- ☐ **Open-Source Money:** Anyone can participate, run nodes, and verify transactions; the system is transparent and deflationary.
- ☐ **Other Innovations:** Stablecoins and central bank digital currencies (CBDCs) offer new digital forms of money, but often reinforce centralization.

The Fork in the Road

Centralized Path: CBDCs could further empower states to control and dilute money.

Decentralized Path: Technologies like Bitcoin allow for open, transparent, and user-governed monetary systems, breaking down financial barriers and empowering individuals.

Key Points

- **Evolution of Money**
  - From barter to commodity money to credit systems and fiat currency.

- **Fractional Reserve Banking Risks**
  - Creates systemic fragility through over-leveraging.

- **Central Banks and Inflation**

- Enable governments to print money, devaluing currency and concentrating wealth.

- **Modern Financial Problems**

  - Inflation, instability, and limited upward mobility globally.

- **Decentralized Alternatives**

  - Bitcoin as open-source, censorship-resistant money with fixed supply.

- **The Fork in the Road**

  - Centralized CBDCs vs. decentralized Bitcoin systems.

Conclusion

The centralized fiat system is fundamentally broken. Bitcoin offers an open, transparent, and user-governed alternative for global financial freedom. Modern money is broken due to centralization, opacity, and corruption. A decentralized, open-source, and transparent monetary system could restore power to individuals and connect people globally.

How Money and Banking Work — And Why They're Broken Today

Watch the related video http://bit.ly/4kjHi2F

Scan QR Code To Watch Video

Chapter 20

Best Places to Buy Bitcoin in the USA (2025 Guide)

Overview

A practical guide for US residents to choose the safest and most suitable Bitcoin buying platforms. This chapter offers a comprehensive guide for Americans on selecting the safest, easiest, and most feature-rich Bitcoin exchanges as of 2025. It highlights platforms to avoid, those suitable for different user types, and details about fees, state restrictions, and custody options.

General Advice

Choose US-Based Exchanges: Avoid international platforms like Ledger or Exodus due to funding and support issues.

State Availability: Ensure the exchange operates in your state; e.g., New York has strict requirements (BitLicense).

Exchange Categories

1. Large Crypto Exchanges

- Examples: Coinbase, Binance, Kraken.
- Pros: High volume, wide range of cryptocurrencies.
- Cons: Overwhelming for Bitcoin buyers, slow support, not Bitcoin-focused.

2. Beginner-Friendly Apps

- Examples: PayPal, Robinhood, Cash App.
- Pros: Easy to use, accessible.
- Cons: Withdrawal limits (e.g., $2,000 max on Cash App), not Bitcoin-focused.

3. Bitcoin-Only Exchanges (Custodial)

- Strike: Simple buying/selling, supports Bitcoin and Lightning Network.
- River: Recurring buys, interest on cash, transparent custody, live support, but you do not hold your Bitcoin until withdrawal.

4. Bitcoin-Only Exchanges (Non-Custodial)

- **Bitcoin Well:** Direct-to-cold-storage purchases, recurring buys, large transactions, strong support. Requires user to have a Bitcoin wallet.
- **Unchained:** All-in-one solution for large purchases and secure storage using multi-signature vaults. US-based support, ideal for inheritance and backup. Requires an account with annual fees.

Fees Overview (as of 2025)

Coinbase: Free account, $10 wire deposit, spread 0.5-0.6%, transaction fees 1-3.99%, network withdrawal fees.

Cash App: Free account, spread 0-1%, transaction fees 0.75-3%, network withdrawal fees plus up to $3.

River: Free account, small spread, transaction fees 0.25-1%, network withdrawal fees.

Bitcoin Well: Free account, 1.2% spread, wire transfers only.

Unchained: $250 account fee, trading fees 1-1.5%, no withdrawal fees, wire transfers only with $2,000 minimum.

Additional Tips

- ☐ **Prioritize User Experience Over Small Fee Differences:** A smooth, secure experience is more important than saving minor fees.
- ☐ **Custody Matters:** Non-custodial solutions (where you hold your Bitcoin) eliminate the risk of losing access due to exchange issues.

To buy Bitcoin in the USA in 2025:

- Stick to US-based, state-compliant exchanges.
- Choose the platform that matches your needs (beginner, large purchases, self-custody).
- Review fee structures, withdrawal limits, and custody options before committing.

Key Points

- **Large Exchanges (e.g. Coinbase, Kraken)**
    - Wide selection but not Bitcoin-focused.

- **Beginner Apps (e.g. Cash App, Robinhood)**
    - Easy to use but with withdrawal limits.

- **Bitcoin-Only Custodial Exchanges (e.g. Strike, River)**
    - Focused services with varying custody setups.

- **Bitcoin-Only Non-Custodial (e.g. Bitcoin Well, Unchained)**
    - Purchases go directly to your own wallet, enhancing security.

- **Fees and Recommendations**
    - Prioritize user experience and security over minor fee differences.

Conclusion

Select state-compliant, user-friendly, and secure platforms aligned with your custody preferences to build a strong Bitcoin position.

Best Places to Buy Bitcoin in the USA (2025 Guide)

Watch the related video http://bit.ly/4nxcNsP

Scan QR Code To Watch Video

Chapter 21

Bitcoin, Broken Money, and the Future of Economic Freedom

Overview

This chapter is a comprehensive documentary-style exploration of the problems with the current monetary system, the impact of inflation and fiat currencies, and the case for Bitcoin as a solution. It covers economic, social, ethical, and spiritual dimensions, featuring personal stories, historical context, and a deep dive into how Bitcoin works and why it matters.

The Broken Fiat Money System

- **Historical Context:** In 1971, the U.S. dollar was decoupled from gold, enabling unlimited money printing to fund wars and government spending.

- **Consequences:**

    - Decades of purchasing power erosion; wages lag behind living costs, trapping people financially.

    - Inflation is mainly monetary (currency expansion) rather than purely physical (supply shocks).

    - The fiat system favors elites, fosters debt dependency, and widens wealth inequality.

    - Individuals are forced to use government-issued money without democratic say in monetary policy.

The Case for Bitcoin

Why Fiat Fails

- **Centralized Control:** Governments and central banks dilute currency value, causing hidden theft via inflation.

- **Economic Instability:** Printing money funds wars and reckless spending, destabilizing societies.

- **Social Consequences:** People delay life milestones (children, homes), and younger generations struggle more than their parents.

Bitcoin's Solution

- **Fixed Supply:** Only 21 million Bitcoin will ever exist, immune to dilution and inflation.

- **Decentralization:** No single entity controls Bitcoin; it runs on a global, trustless, peer-to-peer network.

- **Digital Bearer Asset:** Ownership is secured by cryptographic keys, not dependent on banks or governments.

- **Financial Inclusion:** Anyone with internet access can use Bitcoin, bypassing traditional financial barriers, vital in authoritarian or unstable regions.

Technical Advantages

- **Blockchain:** Transparent, immutable ledger updated globally every ~10 minutes; removes intermediaries.

- **Security & Privacy:** Funds secured by cryptography, immune to arbitrary seizure or censorship.

- **Portability & Divisibility:** Transferable globally within minutes; divisible down to Satoshis; verifiable by anyone.

Bitcoin vs CBDCs (Central Bank Digital Currencies)

- **CBDCs:** Digital fiat currencies controlled by governments, enabling surveillance and transaction censorship.

- **Risks:** Accounts can be frozen, purchases limited, or access denied based on behavior or location (as seen in China).

- **Bitcoin's Advantage:** Permissionless, censorship-resistant, and not programmable for authoritarian control.

Moral, Social, and Religious Perspectives

- **Ethics of Money:** Inflation, debt, and central banking are criticized as unjust in many religious and philosophical traditions.

- **Religious Parallels:**

    - **Islam:** Supports sound money that cannot be created from nothing.
    - **Judaism:** Values decentralization and proof of work.
    - **Buddhism:** Emphasizes validation and decentralized truth.
    - **Christianity:** Warns against unjust monetary systems.

- **Vedic Traditions:** Advocate money serving both material and spiritual well-being.
- **Unifying Force:** Bitcoin is viewed as a tool for justice, equality, and even spiritual growth, bridging divides across politics and religion.

Real-World Impact and Global Use Cases

- **Financial Freedom:** Empowers property rights and wealth preservation in oppressive or unstable regimes.
- **Humanitarian Aid:** Used to bypass banking restrictions during crises (e.g., Ukraine war, aid to Afghan women).
- **Political Resistance:** Enables dissidents and activists to circumvent government financial controls.
- **Adoption in Needful Regions:** High usage in countries with broken currencies or authoritarian governments (e.g., Nigeria, El Salvador).

The Vision for the Future

- **Potential Outcomes:**
  - A Bitcoin standard could reduce wars, shrink government overreach, and foster a savings- and equity-based economy.
  - Bitcoin adoption is accelerating, especially where it is most needed.
  - Transitioning to Bitcoin could end historical cycles of oppression and revolution by removing governments' power to print money.

- **Call to Action:** Advocates for a sound money system built on Bitcoin, emphasizing hope, freedom, and a just, abundant future.

Key Takeaways

- The fiat system is fundamentally flawed, fueling inequality, instability, and loss of personal freedom.

- Bitcoin offers a transparent, fair, and decentralized alternative empowering individuals globally.

- Adoption is both a technological and ethical movement with potential to reshape economies and societies for the better.

Bitcoin, Broken Money, and the Future of Economic Freedom

Watch the related video http://bit.ly/44v6q0d

Scan QR Code To Watch Video

In Conclusion

The Bitcoin Pocket Book provides a straightforward and practical understanding of Bitcoin and its role in the evolving world of digital finance. By breaking down complex terms and processes into simple explanations, it ensures that anyone – regardless of background – can grasp the basics of Bitcoin with confidence.

Throughout the book, readers learn about the origins of Bitcoin, how it operates without traditional banks, and the potential benefits it offers in terms of transparency, security, and financial independence. Practical guidance is provided on how to store, send, and use Bitcoin safely, emphasizing the importance of personal responsibility in managing digital assets.

The video series (Scan QR Codes) in the book also highlights the broader economic and societal impacts of Bitcoin, encouraging readers to think critically about the future of money and how decentralized technologies may influence their personal and professional lives. It presents Bitcoin not just as an investment opportunity but as a tool that could redefine global economic systems.

Overall, *The Bitcoin Pocket Book* equips readers with foundational knowledge to navigate the cryptocurrency landscape with clarity. It serves as a reminder that understanding digital money is no longer optional but essential; empowering readers to embrace innovation and make informed decisions in this rapidly changing financial era.

References

99 Bitcoins. (2015, August 5). *What is Bitcoin Mining for Beginners – Short and Simple [Video]*. YouTube. https://www.youtube.com/watch?v=mrtSAgcpack

Altcoin Daily. (2023, September 17). *The greatest Bitcoin explanation of ALL TIME (in under 10 minutes) [Video]*. YouTube. https://www.youtube.com/watch?v=5JDrK7sP3gA

Binance. (2025, March 26). *What is Bitcoin: The future of money, explained in 4 minutes [Video]*. YouTube. https://www.youtube.com/watch?v=-1ErJsH73Lk

Bitcoin Magazine. (2024, May 2). *Bitcoin: There is no second best | Michael Saylor at Bitcoin for Corporations [Video]*. YouTube. https://www.youtube.com/watch?v=S3T4nhtHxOA

Bitcoin Magazine. (2024, August 2). *Michael Saylor Bitcoin 2024 keynote speech (with slides) [Video]*. YouTube. https://www.youtube.com/watch?v=mOne66vv2QU

Bitcoin Magazine. (2025, May 29). *The math behind $1M Bitcoin by 2028 – Arthur Hayes explains | Bitcoin 2025 [Video]*. YouTube. https://www.youtube.com/watch?v=cTNAX8cZDXY

BTCPrague. (2024, June 18). *Jack Mallers — There is no second best (BTC Prague 2024 keynote) [Video]*. YouTube. https://www.youtube.com/watch?v=--IFcOlEfl4

CoinGecko. (2024, May 16). *Why does Bitcoin have value? Explained in 3 minutes [Video]*. YouTube. https://www.youtube.com/watch?v=Js6qesKGzp8

Cointelegraph. (2025, May 31). *Why Bitcoin could 10x by 2030 – Michael Saylor [Video]*. YouTube. https://www.youtube.com/watch?v=uc28JtZflnA

Darren Honeysett. (2025, January 31). *Where to buy Bitcoin in the USA in 2025 [Video]*. YouTube. https://www.youtube.com/watch?v=vepktoueCHw

From The Desk Of Anthony Pompliano. (2025, June 5). *Big banks continue to capitulate on Bitcoin [Video]*. YouTube. https://www.youtube.com/watch?v=fDP7gm5D-AQ

Lyn Alden Media. (2024, April 28). *How money & banking work (& why they're broken today) – Lyn Alden [Video]*. YouTube. https://www.youtube.com/watch?v=jk_HWmmwiAs

Mark Moss. (2025, March 4). *Will Bitcoin hit $200K? | 5 data signals predicting the market top [Video]*. YouTube. https://www.youtube.com/watch?v=wDokfgGZps4

Mark Moss. (2025, May 6). *The brutal Bitcoin truths I wish I knew sooner! | 15 lessons [Video]*. YouTube. https://www.youtube.com/watch?v=QyaxFLg7_hg

Mark Moss. (2025, June 5). *The hidden formula controlling Bitcoin's price! [Video]*. YouTube. https://www.youtube.com/watch?v=FnkFKQZ4giI

MoneyShow. (2025, June 16). *Why Bitcoin skeptics are about to be proven wrong | Matt Hougan [Video]*. YouTube. https://www.youtube.com/watch?v=c2943HNLYhc

Natalie Brunell. (2025, May 8). *Michael Saylor: 100x return strategy, Bitcoin vs macro panic & the BTC corporate treasury revolution [Video]*. YouTube. https://www.youtube.com/watch?v=hwz5S1rcZ6M

Swan Bitcoin. (2021, November 1). *Bitcoin is generational wealth – A short film [Video]*. YouTube. https://www.youtube.com/watch?v=3Rnqst5qCgA

Swan Bitcoin. (2024, October 24). *Why you won't retire without Bitcoin – The harsh truth [Video]*. YouTube. https://www.youtube.com/watch?v=E7H4ezpLyjk

Swan Bitcoin. (2024, July 25). *God bless Bitcoin | Full movie | Documentary [Video]*. YouTube. https://www.youtube.com/watch?v=oksraL7wN6Q

Made in United States
Cleveland, OH
13 July 2025